D0802209

STUDY OF A FUNCTION
SOLVED EXERCISES

Alessio Mangoni

ISBN: 9798523791765

DR. ALESSIO MANGONI, PHD

Scientist and theoretical particle physicist, researcher on high energy physics and nuclear physics, author of many scientific articles published on international research journals, available at the link:

http://inspirehep.net/author/profile/A.Mangoni.1

https://www.alessiomangoni.it

I edition, June 2021

Contents

Introduction

We recall the key points concerning the study of a function and propose some exercises that are solved by making extensive use of graphics and comments. This book is suitable for all students who have to perform any study of a function.

The tools needed to solve the exercises are, in general: equations, inequalities and their systems, limits and derivatives.

Theoretical concepts

The study of a function consists of several steps to draw its probable graph.

In general you can follow this scheme:

- Determination of the domain D of the function $f(x)$. For this purpose remember the following well known rules:

    1. denominators never null:

    $$\frac{1}{x} \rightarrow x \neq 0\,;$$

    2. arguments with even or fractional in-

dex roots, never negative:

$$\sqrt[n]{x}\,, n \text{ even } \rightarrow\ x \geq 0\,;$$

3. arguments of logarithms are always positive:

$$\log x\ \rightarrow\ x > 0\,;$$

4. arguments of the inverse trigonometric functions arcsin and arccos always between -1 and 1:

$$\arcsin x\,,\ \arccos x\ \rightarrow\ -1 < x < 1\,;$$

- Check for possible symmetries of the function $f(x)$ (even or odd). A function is said to be even if

$$f(-x) = f(x)\,, \forall x\,,$$

while is said to be odd if

$$f(-x) = -f(x), \forall x \, ;$$

- Search for possible points of intersection of the graph of the function $f(x)$ with the Cartesian axes, solving a system with the equation $y = f(x)$, firstly together with the equation of the x axis ($y = 0$), then with the equation of the y axis ($x = 0$);

- Study of the sign of the function $f(x)$, solving the inequality $f(x) > 0$. This allows you to exclude areas of the plane where the graph of the function will certainly not pass (for example if for certain values of x the $f(x)$ is positive, i.e. $y > 0$, then it is necessary to cross, for the tract of the x in question, the part under the abscissa axis);

- Study of the sign of the first derivative $f'(x)$,

solving the inequality $f'(x) > 0$ to find possible maxima and minima. This also allows us to understand when the function $f(x)$ is increasing (if $y' > 0$) and when it is decreasing (if $y' < 0$);

- Search for any asymptotes. There are three types of asymptotes: horizontal, oblique and vertical. Horizontal asymptotes are horizontal lines with an equation of the type $y = q$. There can be none, one or two at most, one for x which tends to infinity and one for x which tends to minus infinity (the two can also coincide). We have the horizontal asymptote $y = q$ if the limit for x which approaches infinity is a finite value q. If this limit were infinite there is no horizontal asymptote, but there could be an oblique one (always in that direction, to be treated separately, x which tends to more or less infinite). There is an oblique asymptote of equation $y = mx + q$ if the limit (for example for x which tends to infinity)

$$\lim_{x \to +\infty} \frac{f(x)}{x} = m \neq 0$$

is a finite value that is not null. In this case, the q intercept is obtained from the limit

$$q = \lim_{x \to +\infty} (f(x) - mx) \ .$$

The existence of the oblique asymptote is verified only if the presence of the horizontal one has been excluded (in the same direction). Possible vertical asymptotes instead occur if an infinite value is obtained from the right and left limits (if allowed according to the domain) for x which tends to points excluded from the domain, but of accumulation for it;

- Study of the sign of the second derivative

$f''(x)$, solving the inequality $f''(x) > 0$ to search for any inflection points and for the areas where the concavity of the function is towards up $(y'' > 0)$ or down $(y'' < 0)$.

When performing the study of a function it is advisable to update the probable graph as you proceed with the next points of the scheme.

Exercise 1

Perform the study of the following function

$$f(x) = x^2 + 3x - 1$$

and plot a qualitative graph on a Cartesian plane of axes (x, y) where $y = f(x)$.

The domain of the function is simply

$$D = \mathbb{R},$$

in fact $f(x)$ is a polynomial of second degree. To find the points of intersection with the abscissa axis we solve the system

$$\begin{cases} y = 0 \\ y = x^2 + 3x - 1 \end{cases},$$

i.e.

$$x^2 + 3x - 1 = 0.$$

The determinant of this second degree equation is

$$\Delta = 3^2 - 4 \cdot (-1) = 13$$

and, being $\Delta > 0$, we have two distinct real solutions

$$x_{1,2} = \frac{-3 \pm \sqrt{13}}{2},$$

or

$$x_1 = \frac{-3 + \sqrt{13}}{2} \simeq 0.303 \,,$$

$$x_2 = \frac{-3 - \sqrt{13}}{2} \simeq -3.303 \,.$$

Therefore the points of intersection with the abscissa axis are

$$P_1 = (x_1, 0) = \left(\frac{-3 + \sqrt{13}}{2}, 0 \right) \simeq (-0.303, 0) \,,$$

$$P_2 = (x_2, 0) = \left(\frac{-3 - \sqrt{13}}{2}, 0 \right) \simeq (-3.303, 0) \,.$$

To find the point of intersection with the ordinate axis we solve the system

$$\begin{cases} x = 0 \\ y = x^2 + 3x - 1 \end{cases} ,$$

which leads to

$$y = -1 \,.$$

The point of intersection with the y-axis is

$$P_3 = (0, -1) \,.$$

The three points found belong to the graph of the function $f(x)$ and they are shown in figure 1.1.

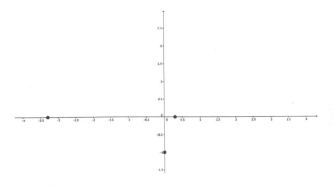

Figure 1.1: Points belonging to the graph of the function $f(x)$.

To verify any symmetries of the function

$$f(x) = x^2 + 3x - 1 \,,$$

we calculate

$$f(-x) = (-x)^2 + 3(-x) - 1 = x^2 - 3x - 1\,,$$

which is neither equal to $f(x)$ nor to $-f(x)$ and therefore the function is neither even nor odd. To study the sign of the function, we solve the inequality

$$x^2 + 3x - 1 > 0\,,$$

from which, being a parabola with upward concavity, it results $y > 0$ if

$$x < x_2 \quad \text{or} \quad x > x_1$$

and therefore the sign of the function follows the scheme shown in figure 1.2.

It is possible to exclude some areas in the Cartesian plane due to the previous results, these areas are shown in figure 1.3.

$x < \frac{-3-\sqrt{13}}{2} \lor x > \frac{-3+\sqrt{13}}{2}$	$\longrightarrow$	$y > 0$
$\frac{-3-\sqrt{13}}{2} < x < \frac{-3+\sqrt{13}}{2}$	$\longrightarrow$	$y < 0$
$x = \frac{-3\pm\sqrt{13}}{2}$	$\longrightarrow$	$y = 0$

Figure 1.2: Sign of the function $f(x)$.

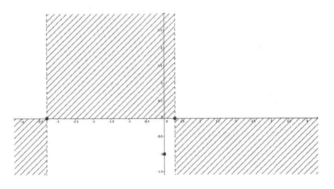

Figure 1.3: Excluded areas for the graph of the function $f(x)$.

The derivative of the function

$$f(x) = x^2 + 3x - 1$$

is

$$f'(x) = 2x + 3$$

and for the study of the sign we solve the inequality

$$2x + 3 > 0,$$

hence $f'(x) > 0$ if

$$x > -\frac{3}{2}.$$

The monotony of the function $f(x)$ can be deduced from the sign of its derivative, in this case we have the trend shown in figure 1.4 and therefore the function $f(x)$ is decreasing if

$$x < -\frac{3}{2},$$

while it is increasing if

$$x > -\frac{3}{2}$$

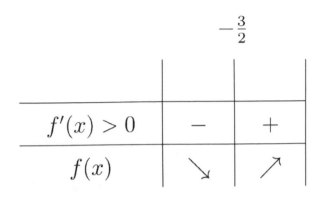

Figure 1.4: Sign of the function $f'(x)$.

and has a relative minimum in

$$x = -\frac{3}{2}.$$

The ordinate of this minimum can be found by calculating

$$f\left(-\frac{3}{2}\right) = \left(-\frac{3}{2}\right)^2 + 3\left(-\frac{3}{2}\right) - 1 = -\frac{13}{4} \simeq -3.25,$$

therefore the relative minimum point (vertex of the parabola) is

$$m = \left(-\frac{3}{2}, -\frac{13}{4}\right) \simeq (-1.5, -3.25).$$

We test the behavior of the function when x tends to $\pm\infty$. In the first case we have

$$\lim_{x \to +\infty} f(x) = \lim_{x \to +\infty} x^2 + 3x - 1 = +\infty$$

while in the second one

$$\lim_{x \to -\infty} f(x) = \lim_{x \to -\infty} x^2 + 3x - 1 = +\infty.$$

There are therefore no horizontal asymptotes. We verify the presence of any oblique asymptotes by calculating

$$\lim_{x \to +\infty} \frac{f(x)}{x} = \lim_{x \to +\infty} \frac{x^2 + 3x - 1}{x}$$

$$= \lim_{x \to +\infty} x + 3 - \frac{1}{x} = +\infty$$

and

$$\lim_{x \to -\infty} \frac{f(x)}{x} = \lim_{x \to -\infty} \frac{x^2 + 3x - 1}{x}$$
$$= \lim_{x \to -\infty} x + 3 - \frac{1}{x} = -\infty \,,$$

which excludes their presence. There can be no vertical asymptotes because there are no points excluded from the domain. We compute the second derivative of the function

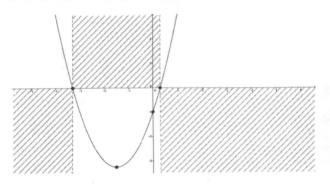

Figure 1.5: Plot of the function $f(x)$.

$$f(x) = x^2 + 3x - 1 \,,$$

i.e.

$$f''(x) = \frac{d}{dx}(2x + 3) = 2 \,,$$

which is always positive,

$$f''(x) > 0 \,, \quad \forall x \in D \,.$$

We conclude that the concavity is always facing upwards (in fact it is a parabola) and that there are no inflection points. Finally, the graph of the function can be drawn qualitatively, as shown in figure 1.5.

Exercise 2

Perform the study of the following function

$$f(x) = \sqrt{x^2 + x}$$

and plot a qualitative graph on a Cartesian plane of axes (x, y) where $y = f(x)$. To calculate the domain of the function it is sufficient to solve the inequality

$$x^2 + x \geq 0\,,$$

i.e.

$$x(x+1) \geq 0.$$

The two factors, $f_1 = x$ and $f_2 = x+1$, are positive if

$$f_1 > 0 \quad \text{if} \quad x > 0$$
$$f_2 > 0 \quad \text{if} \quad x > -1$$

and the sign of the product follows the diagram shown in figure 2.1.

	-1		0	
$x > 0$	$-$		$-$	$+$
$x + 1 > 0$	$-$		$+$	$+$
$x(x+1) > 0$		$+$	$-$	$+$

Figure 2.1: Sign of the function $x(x+1)$.

The domain is therefore

$$D = \{x \in \mathbb{R} : x \leq -1 \text{ or } x \geq 0\}.$$

To find the points of intersection with the x axis we write

$$\begin{cases} y = 0 \\ y = \sqrt{x^2 + x} \end{cases},$$

or simply

$$\sqrt{x^2 + x} = 0.$$

The solutions of this equation are the same of the following equation

$$x^2 + x = x(x + 1) = 0,$$

i.e.

$$\begin{cases} x_1 = 0 \\ x_2 = -1 \end{cases}.$$

The two points of intersection with the abscissa axis are

$$P_1 = (0,0), \quad P_2 = (-1,0).$$

To find the point of intersection with the ordinate axis we solve

$$\begin{cases} x = 0 \\ y = \sqrt{x^2 + x} \end{cases},$$

from which, immediately, $y = 0$, as already known, in fact the intersection with the y-axis can occur at most in a single point, otherwise the curve would not represent a function. The two points of intersection are shown in figure 2.2.

To study the sign of the function, we have to solve the inequality

$$\sqrt{x^2 + x} > 0.$$

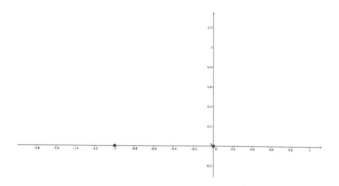

Figure 2.2: Points belonging to the graph of the function $f(x)$.

Being the square root a non-negative quantity (in its domain of definition), the inequality is valid for every x in the domain D such that

$$x \neq 0 \quad \text{and} \quad x \neq -1\,.$$

Comparing this result with the points allowed by the domain we obtain that the function is positive for

$$x < -1 \quad \text{or} \quad x > 0.$$

Figure 2.3 shows the behavior of the sign of the function from which we can exclude some areas in the Cartesian plane. These are shown in fig-

$x < -1 \lor x > 0$	$\longrightarrow$	$y > 0$
$-1 < x < 0$	$\longrightarrow$	$\nexists$
$x = -1 \lor x = 0$	$\longrightarrow$	$y = 0$

Figure 2.3: Sign of the function $f(x)$.

ure 2.4.

The derivative of the function

$$f(x) = \sqrt{x^2 + x} = (x^2 + x)^{1/2}$$

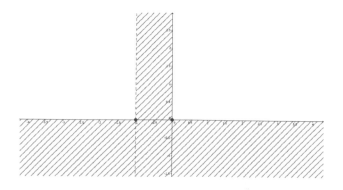

Figure 2.4: Excluded areas for the graph of the function $f(x)$.

is

$$f'(x) = -\frac{1}{2}(x^2 + x)^{-1/2} \cdot (2x),$$

from which

$$f'(x) = \frac{2x + 1}{2\sqrt{x^2 + x}}.$$

To study its sign, we can write

$$\frac{2x + 1}{2\sqrt{x^2 + x}} > 0,$$

therefore for the numerator we have

$$N > 0 \quad \text{if} \quad 2x + 1 > 0 \ \rightarrow \ x > -\frac{1}{2},$$

while for the denominator

$$D > 0 \quad \text{if} \quad 2\sqrt{x^2 + x} > 0 \ \rightarrow \ \sqrt{x^2 + x} > 0$$

and, in particular, the latter relation is true for every x in the domain such that

$$x \neq 0 \quad \text{and} \quad x \neq -1.$$

The sign of the derivative and the behavior of the function $f(x)$, taking into account the domain, is shown in figure 2.5, which shows how the function $f(x)$ is decreasing for $x < -1$ and increasing for $x > 0$.

We now search for the presence of asymptotes.

	-1	$-\frac{1}{2}$	0	
$x + 1/2 > 0$	$-$	$-$	$+$	$+$
$\sqrt{x^2 + x} > 0$	$+$	$+$	$+$	$+$
$\mathcal{D}$	$\exists$	$\nexists$	$\nexists$	$\exists$
$f'(x) = \frac{x+1/2}{\sqrt{x^2+x}} > 0$	$-$			$+$
$f(x)$	$\searrow$			$\nearrow$

Figure 2.5: Sign of the function $f'(x)$.

We calculate the limits

$$\lim_{x \to +\infty} f(x) = \lim_{x \to +\infty} \sqrt{x^2 + x} = +\infty \,,$$

$$\lim_{x \to -\infty} f(x) = \lim_{x \to -\infty} \sqrt{x^2 + x} = +\infty \,,$$

from which can exclude the presence of horizontal asymptotes. We verify the existence of any oblique asymptotes by calculating

$$\lim_{x \to +\infty} \frac{f(x)}{x} = \lim_{x \to +\infty} \frac{\sqrt{x^2 + x}}{x}$$
$$= \lim_{x \to +\infty} \frac{|x|\sqrt{1 + 1/x}}{x}$$
$$= \lim_{x \to +\infty} \frac{|x|}{x} = 1 \, ,$$

in fact, for x which tends towards infinity, the module of x coincides with x itself. We therefore have an oblique (right) asymptote of the form

$$y = mx + q \, ,$$

with angular coefficient

$$m = \lim_{x \to +\infty} \frac{f(x)}{x} = 1 \, .$$

We calculate the value of q with the limit

$$q = \lim_{x \to +\infty} \left(f(x) - mx \right) = \lim_{x \to +\infty} \left(\sqrt{x^2 + x} - x \right)$$

$$= \lim_{x \to +\infty} \left(\sqrt{x^2 + x} - x \right) \frac{\sqrt{x^2 + x} + x}{\sqrt{x^2 + x} + x}$$

$$= \lim_{x \to +\infty} \frac{x^2 + x x^2}{\sqrt{x^2 + x} + x} = \lim_{x \to +\infty} \frac{x}{|x|\sqrt{1 + 1/x} + x}$$

$$= \lim_{x \to +\infty} \frac{1}{\sqrt{1 + 1/x} + 1} = \frac{1}{2} \, .$$

The right oblique asymptote is

$$y = x + \frac{1}{2} \, .$$

Similarly we calculate

$$\lim_{x \to -\infty} \frac{f(x)}{x} = \lim_{x \to -\infty} \frac{\sqrt{x^2 + x}}{x}$$

$$= \lim_{x \to -\infty} \frac{|x|\sqrt{1 + 1/x}}{x}$$

$$= \lim_{x \to -\infty} \frac{|x|}{x} = -1 \, ,$$

in fact, for x which tends to minus infinity, the module of x coincides with the opposite of x. We therefore have an oblique (left) asymptote of the form

$$y = mx + q \,,$$

with angular coefficient

$$m = \lim_{x \to -\infty} \frac{f(x)}{x} = -1 \,.$$

We calculate the value of q with the limit

$$q = \lim_{x \to -\infty} \left(f(x) - mx \right) = \lim_{x \to -\infty} \left(\sqrt{x^2 + x} + x \right)$$

$$= \lim_{x \to -\infty} \left(\sqrt{x^2 + x} + x \right) \frac{\sqrt{x^2 + x} - x}{\sqrt{x^2 + x} - x}$$

$$= \lim_{x \to -\infty} \frac{x^2 + x x^2}{\sqrt{x^2 + x} - x} = \lim_{x \to -\infty} \frac{x}{|x|\sqrt{1 + 1/x} - x}$$

$$= \lim_{x \to -\infty} \frac{1}{-\sqrt{1 + 1/x} - 1} = -\frac{1}{2} \,.$$

The left oblique asymptote is

$$y = -x - \frac{1}{2} \,.$$

To search for any vertical asymptotes we must calculate the limits (right and left) for x which tends to the abscissa of the points excluded from the domain which are accumulation points for it. In this case there are no points with these characteristics, therefore there are no vertical asymptotes. The second derivative of the function

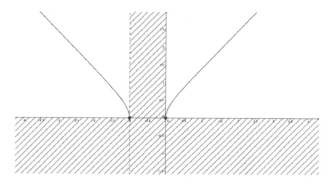

Figure 2.6: Plot of the function $f(x)$.

$$f(x) = \sqrt{x^2 + x} = (x^2 + x)^{1/2}$$

is

$$f''(x) = \frac{d}{dx}\left(\frac{2x+1}{2\sqrt{x^2+x}}\right)$$
$$= \frac{1}{2}\frac{d}{dx}\left((2x+1)(x^2+x)^{-1/2}\right)$$
$$= \frac{1}{2}\left(2(x^2+x)^{-\frac{1}{2}} - \frac{1}{2}(2x+1)^2(x^2+x)^{-\frac{3}{2}}\right)$$
$$= \frac{1}{4(x^2+x)^{3/2}}\left(4(x^2+x) - (2x+1)^2\right)$$
$$= \frac{1}{4(x^2+x)^{3/2}}\left(4x^2+4x-4x^2-1-4x\right),$$

from which

$$f''(x) = -\frac{1}{4(x^2+x)^{3/2}}\,.$$

To study its sign, it is necessary to solve the inequality

$$-\frac{1}{4(x^2+x)^{3/2}} > 0\,.$$

We immediately observe that the quantity on the first member is always negative in the domain D, in fact the denominator of the fraction is always positive (in its domain of definition). We therefore conclude that the concavity of the graph of the function is always pointing downwards and there are no inflection points. The function graph can be drawn qualitatively and is shown in figure 2.6.

Exercise 3

Perform the study of the following function

$$\sin(x^2 + 1)$$

and draw a qualitative graph for

$$0 \leq x^2 + 1 \leq 2\pi \,,$$

on a system of Cartesian axes (x, y) where $y = f(x)$. Its domain can be obtained by considering only the given condition, in fact there are no further points to be excluded. Starting from

$$0 \le x^2 + 1 \le 2\pi \,,$$

we have the inequality

$$x^2 \ge -1 \,,$$

that is always satisfied and

$$x^2 \le 2\pi - 1 \,,$$

which leads to

$$-\sqrt{2\pi - 1} \le x \le \sqrt{2\pi - 1} \,.$$

The domain is therefore

$$D = \left[-\sqrt{2\pi - 1}, \sqrt{2\pi - 1} \right] \,.$$

To find the points of intersection with the x axis we can consider the system

$$\begin{cases} y = 0 \\ y = \sin(x^2 + 1) \end{cases},$$

which leads to the equation

$$\sin(x^2 + 1) = 0.$$

The function $\sin x$ for x belonging to the domain cancels when its argument takes the values

$$x = 0,\ \pi,\ 2\pi.$$

Therefore, the following three equations must be solved

$$x^2 + 1 = 0, \tag{3.1}$$

$$x^2 + 1 = \pi, \tag{3.2}$$

$$x^2 + 1 = 2\pi. \tag{3.3}$$

The first one has no real solutions, while the last two lead to the following four abscissas

$$x_1 = \sqrt{\pi - 1}, \tag{3.4}$$

$$x_2 = -\sqrt{\pi - 1}, \tag{3.5}$$

$$x_3 = \sqrt{2\pi - 1}, \tag{3.6}$$

$$x_4 = -\sqrt{2\pi - 1}. \tag{3.7}$$

The four points of intersection with the abscissa axis are

$$P_1 = \left(\sqrt{\pi - 1}, 0\right) \simeq (1.463, 0), \tag{3.8}$$

$$P_2 = \left(-\sqrt{\pi - 1}, 0\right) \simeq (-1.463, 0), \tag{3.9}$$

$$P_3 = \left(\sqrt{2\pi - 1}, 0\right) \simeq (2.299, 0), \tag{3.10}$$

$$P_4 = \left(-\sqrt{2\pi - 1}, 0\right) \simeq (-2.299, 0). \tag{3.11}$$

To find the points of intersection with the y axis, we solve the system

$$\begin{cases} x = 0 \\ y = \sin(x^2 + 1) \end{cases},$$

from which

$$y = \sin(1) \simeq 0.841 \,.$$

The point of intersection with the y axis is therefore

$$P_5 = (0, \sin 1) \simeq (0, 0.841) \,.$$

The five points of intersection with the two Cartesian axes are shown in figure 3.1.

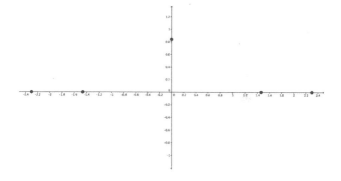

Figure 3.1: Points belonging to the graph of the function $f(x)$.

The function is even, in fact

$$f(-x) = \sin\left((-x)^2 + 1\right) = \sin(x^2 + 1) = f(x)$$

and its graph is therefore symmetrical with respect to the ordinate axis. To study the sign of the function we have to solve the inequality

$$\sin(x^2 + 1) > 0\,.$$

The solutions of this inequality are the x that satisfy

$$0 < x^2 + 1 < \pi\,,$$

the first inequality is always satisfied

$$x^2 + 1 > 0\,,$$

and we have to solve

$$x^2 + 1 < \pi\,, \quad x^2 < \pi - 1\,,$$

hence the solution

$$-\sqrt{\pi - 1} < x < \sqrt{\pi - 1}.$$

Figure 3.2 shows the behavior of the sign of the function from which we can exclude some areas of the Cartesian plane, as shown in figure 3.3.

$-\sqrt{\pi - 1} < x < \sqrt{\pi - 1}$	$\longrightarrow$	$y > 0$
$-\sqrt{2\pi - 1} < x < -\sqrt{\pi - 1}$	$\longrightarrow$	$y < 0$
$\sqrt{\pi - 1} < x < \sqrt{2\pi - 1}$	$\longrightarrow$	$y < 0$
$x = \pm\sqrt{\pi - 1}$	$\longrightarrow$	$y = 0$
$x = \pm\sqrt{2\pi - 1}$	$\longrightarrow$	$y = 0$

Figure 3.2: Sign of the function $f(x)$.

The derivative of the function

$$\sin(x^2 + 1)$$

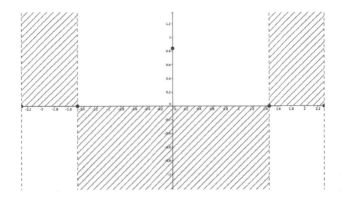

Figure 3.3: Excluded areas for the graph of the function $f(x)$.

is

$$f'(x) = \cos(x^2 + 1) \cdot 2x \, .$$

Its sign can be studied by solving the inequality

$$\cos(x^2 + 1) \cdot 2x > 0 \, ,$$

The second factor is positive if $x > 0$, while the first factor is positive if

$$\cos(x^2 + 1) > 0\,,$$

i.e. if

$$0 < x^2 + 1 < \frac{\pi}{2} \text{ or } \frac{3\pi}{2} < x^2 + 1 < 2\pi\,.$$

We start with the resolution of the first part

$$x^2 + 1 < \frac{\pi}{2}\,, \quad x^2 < \frac{\pi}{2} - 1\,,$$

from which

$$-\sqrt{\pi/2 - 1} < x < \sqrt{\pi/2 - 1}\,.$$

For the second part we have the equivalent system

$$\begin{cases} x^2 + 1 > \frac{3\pi}{2} \\ x^2 + 1 < 2\pi \end{cases}, \quad \begin{cases} x^2 > \frac{3\pi}{2} - 1 \\ x^2 < 2\pi - 1 \end{cases},$$

i.e.

$$\begin{cases} x < -\sqrt{3\pi/2 - 1} \text{ or } x > \sqrt{3\pi/2 - 1} \\ -\sqrt{2\pi - 1} < x < \sqrt{2\pi - 1} \end{cases}.$$

This system has the solution

$$-\sqrt{2\pi - 1} < x < -\sqrt{3\pi/2 - 1} \,,$$

or

$$\sqrt{3\pi/2 - 1} < x < \sqrt{2\pi - 1} \,,$$

which together with what we found before, indicates the values of x for which the first factor of the initial inequality is positive. The sign of that inequality and the behavior of the function $f(x)$ are indicated in figure 3.4, where, for convenience, we report the following values

$$A = \sqrt{2\pi - 1} \simeq 2.299 \,, \quad B = \sqrt{3\pi/2 - 1} \simeq 1.927$$
$$C = \sqrt{\pi/2 - 1} \simeq 0.756 \,.$$

	$-A$	$-B$	$-C$	0	C	B	A
$\cos(x^2+1)>0$		$+$	$-$	$+$	$+$	$-$	$+$
$2x>0$		$-$	$-$	$-$	$+$	$+$	$+$
$2x\cos(x^2+1)>0$		$-$	$+$	$-$	$+$	$-$	$+$
$f(x)$		↘	↗	↘	↗	↘	↗

Figure 3.4: Sign of the function $f'(x)$.

The function $f(x)$, in its domain

$$D = \left[-\sqrt{2\pi - 1}, \sqrt{2\pi - 1}\right] = [-A, A]\,,$$

is decreasing below the minimum of abscissa

$$x = -\sqrt{3\pi/2 - 1}\,,$$

it is increasing from that point to the maximum of abscissa

$$x = -\sqrt{\pi/2 - 1}\,,$$

then it is again decreasing until the second minimum at $x = 0$ and similarly symmetrically to the right of the origin (the function is even). The three points of relative minimum are

$$m_1 = \left(-\sqrt{3\pi/2 - 1}, \sin(3\pi/2)\right) \simeq (-1.927, -1),$$

$$m_2 = (0, \sin 1) \simeq (0, 0.841),$$

$$m_1 = \left(\sqrt{3\pi/2 - 1}, \sin(3\pi/2)\right) \simeq (1.927, -1),$$

The two points of relative maximum are instead

$$M_1 = \left(-\sqrt{\pi/2 - 1}, \sin(\pi/2)\right) \simeq (-0.756.1),$$

$$M_2 = \left(\sqrt{\pi/2 - 1}, \sin(\pi/2)\right) \simeq (0.756, 1).$$

There can be no horizontal or oblique asymptotes, because the domain is a limited range of the real axis. The same applies to vertical asymptotes, in fact there are no points excluded from the domain, we remember that D is a closed interval. We compute the second derivative of the function

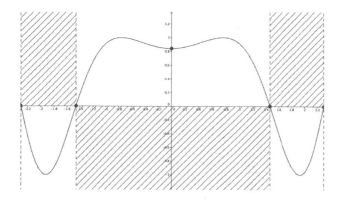

Figure 3.5: Plot of the function $f(x)$.

$$\sin(x^2 + 1)$$

by writing

$$
\begin{aligned}
f''(x) &= \frac{d}{dx}\left(\cos(x^2 + 1) \cdot 2x\right) \\
&= 2\left(\cos(x^2 + 1) - 2x^2 \sin(x^2 + 1)\right) .
\end{aligned}
$$

To study its sign we consider the inequality

$$2\left(\cos(x^2 + 1) - 2x^2 \sin(x^2 + 1)\right) > 0 \, ,$$

that is equivalent to

$$\cos(x^2 + 1) - 2x^2 \sin(x^2 + 1) > 0\,.$$

This inequality cannot be solved exactly, we trace a qualitative trend with the results obtained so far, which we show in figure 3.5.

Exercise 4

Perform the study of the following function

$$f(x) = e^x \cdot 2^{x^2}$$

and plot a qualitative graph on a Cartesian plane of axes (x, y) where $y = f(x)$. The domain of the function is

$$D = \mathbb{R}.$$

To find the points of intersection with the abscissa axis we solve the system

$$\begin{cases} y = 0 \\ y = e^x \cdot 2^{x^2} \end{cases},$$

i.e.

$$e^x \cdot 2^{x^2} = 0,$$

which obviously does not admit solutions, since the two exponential functions are always positive. There are therefore no points of intersection with the abscissa axis. For the point of intersection with the ordinate axis, we solve the system

$$\begin{cases} x = 0 \\ y = e^x \cdot 2^{x^2} \end{cases},$$

which quickly leads to

$$y = 1.$$

The point of intersection with the y-axis is

$$P_1 = (0.1)$$

and it is shown in figure 4.1.

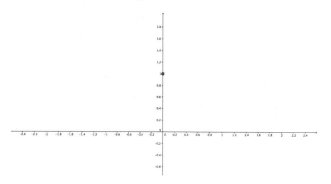

Figure 4.1: Point belonging to the graph of the function $f(x)$.

To verify any symmetries of the function

$$f(x) = e^x \cdot 2^{x^2}$$

we calculate

$$f(-x) = e^{(-x)} \cdot 2^{(-x)^2} = e^{(-x)} \cdot 2^{x^2}$$

and we conclude that the function is neither even nor odd. To study the sign of the function, we solve the inequality

$$e^x \cdot 2^{x^2} > 0$$

which is always satisfied as previously mentioned. The part of the Cartesian plane with $y < 0$ can be totally excluded, as is shown in figure 4.2. To calculate the derivative of the function

$$f(x) = e^x \cdot 2^{x^2}$$

note that we can write

$$\frac{d}{dx} \ln\left(2^{x^2}\right) = \frac{1}{2^{x^2}} \cdot \frac{d}{dx}\left(2^{x^2}\right)$$

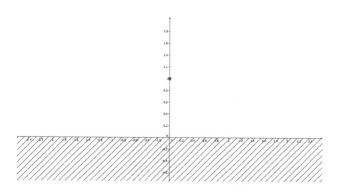

Figure 4.2: Excluded areas for the graph of the function $f(x)$.

with

$$\ln\left(2^{x^2}\right) = x^2 \ln 2\,,$$

from which

$$\frac{d}{dx}\left(2^{x^2}\right) = 2^{x^2}\frac{d}{dx}\ln\left(2^{x^2}\right) = 2^{x^2}2x\ln 2\,.$$

The derivative of the function is

$$f'(x) = e^x \cdot 2^{x^2} + 2xe^x\,2^{x^2}\ln 2 = e^x\,2^{x^2}(1+2x\ln 2)\,.$$

The study of the sign of $f'(x)$ can be done by solving the inequality

$$e^x \, 2^{x^2} (1 + 2x \ln 2) > 0 \,,$$

from which, thanks to the considerations made previously on the sign of exponentials,

$$1 + 2x \ln 2 > 0 \,,$$

i.e.

$$x > -\frac{1}{2 \ln 2} \,.$$

The monotony of the function $f(x)$ can be deduced from the sign of its first derivative and the trend is shown in figure 4.3.

We observe that the function $f(x)$ is decreasing for

$$x < -\frac{1}{2 \ln 2} \,,$$

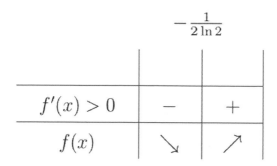

Figure 4.3: Sign of the function $f'(x)$.

increasing for

$$x > -\frac{1}{2\ln 2}$$

and has a minimum in

$$x = -\frac{1}{2\ln 2} \simeq -0.721 \, .$$

The ordinate of the minimum point is

$$f\left(-\frac{1}{2\ln 2}\right) = e^{\left(-\frac{1}{2\ln 2}\right)} \cdot 2^{\left(-\frac{1}{2\ln 2}\right)^2} \simeq 0.697 \, ,$$

therefore the minimum point is

$$m \simeq (-0.721, 0.697).$$

We verify the presence of horizontal asymptotes by calculating the limit

$$\lim_{x \to +\infty} f(x) = \lim_{x \to +\infty} e^x \cdot 2^{x^2} = +\infty$$

which excludes the presence of a right horizontal asymptote. We then calculate

$$\lim_{x \to +\infty} \frac{f(x)}{x} = \lim_{x \to +\infty} \frac{e^x \cdot 2^{x^2}}{x} = +\infty \,,$$

in fact, exponentials diverge faster than powers of x. Therefore there is not even an oblique asymptote for x which tends to infinity. We need to calculate the other limit

$$\lim_{x \to -\infty} f(x) = \lim_{x \to -\infty} e^x \cdot 2^{x^2} \,,$$

which appears as an indeterminate form. We can write, with a change of variable,

$$\lim_{x \to -\infty} e^x \cdot 2^{x^2} = \lim_{x \to +\infty} e^{-x} \cdot 2^{(-x)^2}$$

$$= \lim_{x \to +\infty} \frac{2^{x^2}}{e^x} = \lim_{x \to +\infty} \left(\frac{2^x}{e} \right)^x = +\infty \,.$$

Similarly

$$\lim_{x \to -\infty} \frac{f(x)}{x} = \lim_{x \to -\infty} \frac{e^x \cdot 2^{x^2}}{x} = \lim_{x \to +\infty} \frac{2^{x^2}}{xe^x}$$

$$= \lim_{x \to +\infty} \frac{1}{x} \left(\frac{2^x}{e} \right)^x = +\infty$$

and there are neither horizontal nor oblique asymptotes. We calculate the second derivative of the function

$$f(x) = e^x \cdot 2^{x^2} \,,$$

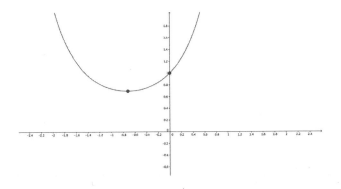

Figure 4.4: Plot of the function $f(x)$.

obtaining

$$
\begin{aligned}
f''(x) = \frac{d}{dx} f'(x) &= \frac{d}{dx} \left(e^x \, 2^{x^2} (1 + 2x \ln 2) \right) \\
&= (1 + 2x \ln 2) \frac{d}{dx} \left(e^x \, 2^{x^2} \right) \\
&+ e^x \, 2^{x^2} (2 \ln 2) = (1 + 2x \ln 2) \\
&\cdot \left(e^x \, 2^{x^2} (1 + 2x \ln 2) \right) + e^x \, 2^{x^2} \\
&\cdot (2 \ln 2) = e^x \, 2^{x^2} \left((1 + 2x \ln 2)^2 \right. \\
&\left. + 2 \ln 2 \right).
\end{aligned}
$$

For the study of its sign we solve the inequality

$$e^x \, 2^{x^2} \left((1 + 2x \ln 2)^2 + 2 \ln 2 \right) > 0 \,,$$

or

$$(1 + 2x \ln 2)^2 + 2 \ln 2 > 0 \,,$$
$$(1 + 2x \ln 2)^2 > -2 \ln 2 \,,$$

which is always satisfied, in fact the first member is a square, which is always non-negative, while the second member is a negative quantity. The $f(x)$ function has always upward concavity and has no inflection points. The graph can be drawn qualitatively as shown in figure 4.4.

Exercise 5

Perform the study of the following function

$$f(x) = 5 \ln \left(\frac{x^2}{2} \right) \, ,$$

and plot a qualitative graph on a Cartesian plane of axes (x, y) where $y = f(x)$. For the domain of the function we observe that the logarithm argument must be positive, in the field of real numbers, hence

$$\frac{x^2}{2} > 0 \, ,$$

which is satisfied by any real x with the exception of $x = 0$. The domain is

$$D = \mathbb{R} - \{0\}\,.$$

For the points of intersection with the abscissa axis, we solve the system

$$\begin{cases} y = 0 \\ y = 5\ln\left(\frac{x^2}{2}\right) \end{cases},$$

i.e.

$$5\ln\left(\frac{x^2}{2}\right) = 0\,.$$

The natural logarithm is zero when its argument assumes the value 1. We have to solve the equation

$$\frac{x^2}{2} = 1\,,$$

from which

$$x_{1,2} = \pm\sqrt{2}\,.$$

The two points of intersection with the abscissa axis are

$$P_1 = (x_2, 0) = (-\sqrt{2}, 0) \simeq (-1,414, 0)\,,$$
$$P_2 = (x_1, 0) = (\sqrt{2}, 0) \simeq (1,414, 0)\,,$$

This function cannot intersect the ordinate axis because $x = 0$ is an excluded point from the domain. The two points of intersection with the x axis are shown in figure 5.1.

To search for possible symmetries we calculate

$$f(-x) = 5\ln\left(\frac{(-x)^2}{2}\right) = 5\ln\left(\frac{x^2}{2}\right) = f(x)$$

and the function is therefore even. Its graph is symmetrical with respect to the ordinate axis. To study the sign of the function, we solve the fol-

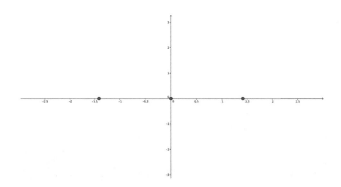

Figure 5.1: Points belonging to the graph of the function $f(x)$.

lowing inequality

$$5 \ln \left(\frac{x^2}{2} \right) > 0 \,,$$

or

$$\frac{x^2}{2} > 1 \,, \quad x^2 - 2 > 0 \,.$$

The parabola associated with the first member of the inequality has an upward concavity and assumes positive values for

$$x < x_1 \quad \text{or} \quad x > x_2\,,$$

with

$$x_{1,2} = \pm\sqrt{2}\,.$$

The Sign of the function $f(x)$ follows the pattern reported in figure 5.2.

$x < -\sqrt{2} \ \lor \ x > \sqrt{2}$	$\longrightarrow$	$y > 0$
$-\sqrt{2} < x < \sqrt{2}$	$\longrightarrow$	$y < 0$
$x = \pm\sqrt{2}$	$\longrightarrow$	$y = 0$

Figure 5.2: Sign of the function $f(x)$.

It is possible to exclude some areas in the Cartesian plan, as shown in figure 5.3.

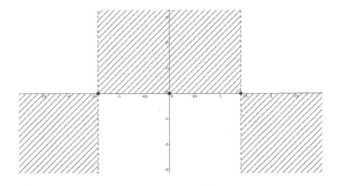

Figure 5.3: Excluded areas for the graph of the function $f(x)$.

The derivative of the function

$$f(x) = 5 \ln \left(\frac{x^2}{2} \right)$$

is

$$f'(x) = 5 \frac{1}{x^2/2} \left(\frac{1}{2} 2x \right) = \frac{10}{x}$$

and to study its sign we have to solve the inequality

$$\frac{10}{x} > 0\,,$$

from which

$$x > 0\,.$$

The monotony of the function $f(x)$ can be deduced from the sign of its derivative, in this case we have the behavior indicated in figure 5.4.

The function $f(x)$ is decreasing for $x < 0$ and increasing for $x > 0$. To search for any asymptotes we calculate

$$\lim_{x \to \pm\infty} f(x) = \lim_{x \to \pm\infty} 5\ln\left(\frac{x^2}{2}\right) = +\infty\,,$$

which excludes the presence of horizontal asymptotes. We also calculate

$$\lim_{x \to \pm\infty} \frac{f(x)}{x} = \lim_{x \to \pm\infty} \frac{5}{x}\ln\left(\frac{x^2}{2}\right)\,.$$

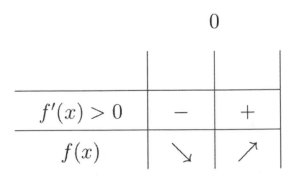

Figure 5.4: Sign of the function $f'(x)$.

We use de L'Hopital's theorem for the indeterminate form $\left(\frac{\infty}{\infty}\right)$, obtaining

$$\lim_{x \to \pm\infty} \frac{5}{x} \ln\left(\frac{x^2}{2}\right) = \lim_{x \to \pm\infty} \frac{10}{x} = 0 \,.$$

From these results we conclude that there are no oblique asymptotes. For the search of vertical asymptotes we calculate the limits

$$\lim_{x \to 0^+} f(x) = \lim_{x \to 0^+} \ln \left(\frac{x^2}{2} \right) = -\infty \,,$$

$$\lim_{x \to 0^-} f(x) = \lim_{x \to 0^-} \ln \left(\frac{x^2}{2} \right) = -\infty \,,$$

which are equal (even function). Therefore the line of equation

$$x = 0$$

represents a vertical asymptote for the function $f(x)$. We calculate the second derivative of the function

$$f(x) = 5 \ln \left(\frac{x^2}{2} \right) \,,$$

as follows

$$f''(x) = \frac{d}{dx} f'(x) = \frac{d}{dx} \left(\frac{10}{x} \right) = -\frac{10}{x^2} \,.$$

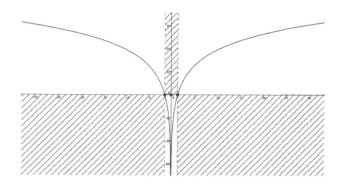

Figure 5.5: Plot of the function $f(x)$.

The second derivative is always negative, in fact the inequality

$$-\frac{10}{x^2} > 0$$

does not allow solutions for x belonging to the domain. The graph of the $f(x)$ function has downward concavity and has no inflection points. Its graph, drawn qualitatively, is shown in figure 5.5.

Exercise 6

Perform the study of the following function

$$f(x) = \frac{x+1}{x-1}$$

and plot a qualitative graph on a Cartesian plane of axes (x, y) where $y = f(x)$. For the domain we write

$$x - 1 \neq 0$$

so that

$$D = \mathbb{R} - \{1\}.$$

For the points of intersection with the abscissa axis we solve the system

$$\begin{cases} y = 0 \\ y = \frac{x+1}{x-1} \end{cases},$$

i.e.

$$\frac{x+1}{x-1} = 0,$$

which admits the solution

$$x = -1.$$

The graph of the function intersects the abscissa axis at the point

$$P_1 = (-1, 0).$$

similarly, we solve the following system for the point of intersection with the ordinate axis

$$\begin{cases} x = 0 \\ y = \frac{x+1}{x-1} \end{cases},$$

which leads to

$$y = -1$$

and the point of intersection with the y axis is

$$P_2 = (0, -1).$$

The two points of intersection are shown in figure 6.1.

We calculate

$$f(-x) = \frac{-x+1}{-x-1} = \frac{x-1}{x+1},$$

which coincides neither with $f(x)$ nor with $-f(-x)$ and therefore the function is neither even nor odd.

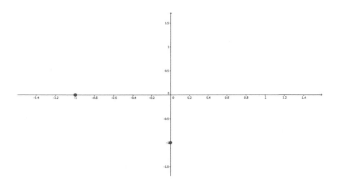

Figure 6.1: Points belonging to the graph of the function $f(x)$.

To study the sign of the function, we consider the inequality

$$\frac{x+1}{x-1} > 0.$$

Considering the numerator and denominator separately, there are two inequalities, the first is

$$x + 1 > 0,$$

with the solution

$$x > -1 \,,$$

while for the second, related to the denominator, i.e.

$$x - 1 > 0$$

we obtain

$$x > 1 \,.$$

A scheme concerning the sign of the function is shown in figure 6.2.

The areas of the Cartesian plane where the function will not pass are shown in figure 6.3.

The derivative of the function

$$f(x) = \frac{x + 1}{x - 1}$$

	-1	1	
$x + 1 > 0$	$-$	$+$	$+$
$x - 1 > 0$	$-$	$-$	$+$
$\frac{x+1}{x-1} > 0$	$+$	$-$	$+$

Figure 6.2: Sign of the function $f(x)$.

is

$$f'(x) = \frac{x - 1 - (x + 1)}{(x - 1)^2} = -\frac{2}{(x - 1)^2} \, ,$$

and its sign can be studied by solving the inequality

$$-\frac{2}{(x - 1)^2} > 0 \, ,$$

which does not admit solutions, in fact the first member quantity is always negative and the func-

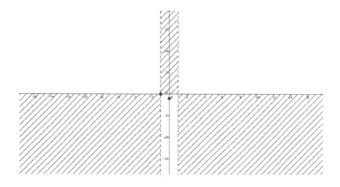

Figure 6.3: Excluded areas for the graph of the function $f(x)$.

tion will always be decreasing as shown in the diagram in figure 6.4.

For the calculation of limits we can write

$$\lim_{x \to \pm\infty} f(x) = \lim_{x \to \pm\infty} \frac{x+1}{x-1} = 1\,,$$

therefore the line of equation

$$y = 1$$

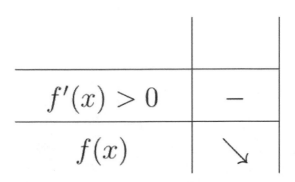

Figure 6.4: Sign of the function $f'(x)$.

represents a horizontal asymptote for the function. We now calculate the limits to the point excluded from the domain

$$\lim_{x \to 1^+} f(x) = \lim_{x \to 1^+} \frac{x+1}{x-1} = \frac{2}{0^+} = +\infty \,,$$

$$\lim_{x \to 1^-} f(x) = \lim_{x \to 1^-} \frac{x+1}{x-1} = \frac{2}{0^-} = -\infty$$

and therefore the line of equation

$$x = 1$$

represents a vertical asymptote. We calculate the second derivative of the function

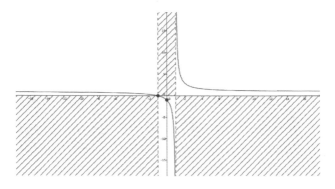

Figure 6.5: Plot of the function $f(x)$.

$$f(x) = \frac{x+1}{x-1},$$

that has the form

$$f''(x) = \frac{d}{dx}f'(x) = \frac{d}{dx}\left(-\frac{2}{(x-1)^2}\right)$$
$$= -2\frac{d}{dx}\left(\frac{1}{(x-1)^2}\right)$$
$$= \frac{4(x-1)}{(x-1)^4} = \frac{4}{(x-1)^3}.$$

We study its sign

$$\frac{4}{(x-1)^3} > 0 \,,$$

which is equivalent to

$$x - 1 > 0 \,,$$

from which

$$x > 1$$

Since the number 1 is excluded from the domain, we conclude that the graph of the function $f(x)$ has the concavity upwards for $x > 1$ and downwards for $x < 1$, as can be observed tracing the qualitative graph, shown in figure 6.5.

Exercise 7

Perform the study of the following function

$$f(x) = \frac{x}{x^2 + 1}$$

and plot a qualitative graph on a Cartesian plane of axes (x, y) where $y = f(x)$. For the domain we request

$$x^2 + 1 \neq 0 \,,$$

which is always satisfied for every real x. The domain is

$$D = \mathbb{R}.$$

To find the points of intersection with the abscissa axis we solve the system

$$\begin{cases} y = 0 \\ y = \frac{x}{x^2+1} \end{cases},$$

or

$$\frac{x}{x^2 + 1} = 0,$$

hence, trivially,

$$x = 0.$$

The plot of the function intersects the abscissa axis at the origin

$$P_1 = (0, 0)$$

which is also the point of intersection with the ordinate axis, as shown in figure 7.1.

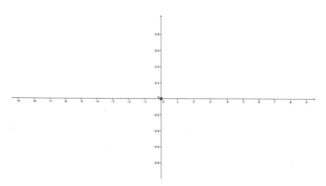

Figure 7.1: Points belonging to the graph of the function $f(x)$.

To study the sign of the function, we have to solve

$$\frac{x}{x^2 + 1} > 0 \,.$$

The denominator is always positive so the inequality becomes

$$x > 0$$

and the sign of the function follows the diagram shown in figure 7.2.

$$0$$

$x > 0$	$-$	$+$
$x^2 + 1 > 0$	$+$	$+$
$\frac{x}{x^2+1} > 0$	$-$	$+$

Figure 7.2: Sign of the function $f(x)$.

The areas of the Cartesian plane where the function does not pass are shown in figure 7.3.

We study the parity of the function by calculating

$$f(-x) = \frac{-x}{(-x)^2 + 1} = -\frac{x}{x^2 + 1} = -f(x),$$

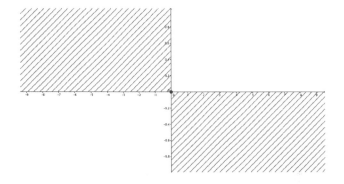

Figure 7.3: Excluded areas for the graph of the function $f(x)$.

from which we deduce that the function is odd and its graph will be symmetrical with respect to the origin. This result could also be predicted by observing that the function is given by the ratio between an odd function and an even function. The derivative of the function

$$f(x) = \frac{x}{x^2 + 1}$$

is as follows

$$f'(x) = \frac{x^2 + 1 - 2x^2}{(x^2 + 1)^2} = \frac{1 - x^2}{(x^2 + 1)^2}.$$

The denominator is always positive and therefore the inequality to be solved to study the sign of f' can be written as

$$1 - x^2 > 0,$$

with the solution

$$-1 < x < 1.$$

The sign of the derivative of the function and the trend of $f(x)$ are shown, respectively, in figures 7.4 and 7.5.

In particular, $f(x)$ has a minimum and a maximum for values of $x = -1$ and $x = 1$, respectively. The ordinate of the minimum is

$$f(-1) = \frac{-1}{(-1)^2 + 1} = -\frac{1}{2},$$

	-1		1	
$1 - x^2 > 0$	$-$	$+$	$-$
$(x^2 + 1)^2 > 0$	$+$	$+$	$+$
$\frac{1-x^2}{(x^2+1)^2} > 0$	$-$	$+$	$-$

Figure 7.4: Sign of the function $f'(x)$.

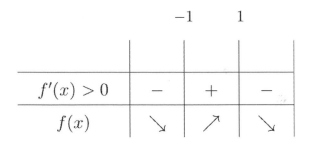

Figure 7.5: Sign of the function $f'(x)$.

while that of the maximum is

$$f(1) = \frac{1}{1^2 + 1} = \frac{1}{2}.$$

Therefore the minimum and maximum points are

$$m = \left(-1, -\frac{1}{2}\right),$$

$$M = \left(1, \frac{1}{2}\right).$$

We calculate now the limits

$$\lim_{x \to \pm\infty} f(x) = \lim_{x \to \pm\infty} \frac{x}{x^2 + 1} = 0,$$

in fact the numerator is a polynomial of lower degree than the denominator. There can be no vertical asymptotes because the domain is the whole field of reals. We calculate the second derivative of the function

$$f(x) = \frac{x}{x^2 + 1},$$

obtaining

$$f''(x) = \frac{d}{dx} f'(x) = \frac{d}{dx} \left(\frac{1 - x^2}{(x^2 + 1)^2} \right)$$

$$= \left(\frac{-2x(x^2 + 1)^2 - 2(x^2 + 1)(2x)(1 - x^2)}{(x^2 + 1)^4} \right)$$

$$= -2 \left(\frac{x(x^2 + 1) + (2x)(1 - x^2)}{(x^2 + 1)^3} \right)$$

$$= -2 \left(\frac{3x - x^3}{(x^2 + 1)^3} \right) = -2x \left(\frac{3 - x^2}{(x^2 + 1)^3} \right).$$

The study of its sign can be done by solving

$$-2x \left(\frac{3 - x^2}{(x^2 + 1)^3} \right) > 0.$$

Note that the denominator of the fraction inside the brackets is always positive. So we can write

$$-x(3 - x^2) > 0.$$

We study the sign of this product, solving the first inequality

$$-x > 0,$$

i.e.

$$x < 0$$

and then the second inequality

$$3 - x^2 > 0 \, ,$$

which has the solution

$$-\sqrt{3} < x < \sqrt{3}$$

The second derivative of the function $f(x)$ is therefore positive for

$$-\sqrt{3} < x < 0 \quad \text{or} \quad x > \sqrt{3}$$

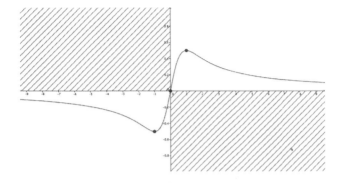

Figure 7.6: Plot of the function $f(x)$.

The function admits three inflection points of abscissas

$$x_{F_1} = -\sqrt{3}\,,$$
$$x_{F_2} = 0\,,$$
$$x_{F_3} = \sqrt{3}\,.$$

The corresponding ordinates are

$$f\left(-\sqrt{3}\right) = \frac{-\sqrt{3}}{3+1} = -\frac{\sqrt{3}}{4} \simeq -0.433\,,$$
$$f\left(0\right) = \frac{0}{0^2+1} = 0\,,$$
$$f\left(\sqrt{3}\right) = \frac{\sqrt{3}}{3+1} = \frac{\sqrt{3}}{4} \simeq 0.433\,.$$

therefore the three points of inflection, where the change of concavity occurs, are

$$F_1 = \left(-\sqrt{3}, -\frac{\sqrt{3}}{4}\right)\,,$$
$$F_2 = (0, 0)\,,$$
$$F_1 = \left(\sqrt{3}, \frac{\sqrt{3}}{4}\right)\,.$$

In particular, the graph of the function $f(x)$ has downward concavity up to the first inflection, then upward concavity up to the origin (second inflection), then downward concavity up to the third inflection and then upward concavity again. The function graph is shown in figure 7.6.

Exercise 8

Perform the study of the following function

$$f(x) = x^{3/2} - x^{-3/2}$$

and plot a qualitative graph on a Cartesian plane of axes (x, y) where $y = f(x)$. The function can also be written as

$$f(x) = \sqrt{x^3} - \frac{1}{\sqrt{x^3}}$$

and its domain can be found by solving the system

$$\begin{cases} x^3 \geq 0 \\ \sqrt{x^3} \neq 0 \end{cases},$$

which has solution

$$x > 0$$

and therefore the domain is

$$D = \mathbb{R}^+.$$

To find the points of intersection with the abscissa axis we solve the system

$$\begin{cases} y = 0 \\ y = x^{3/2} - x^{-3/2} \end{cases},$$

or

$$\sqrt{x^3} - \frac{1}{\sqrt{x^3}} = 0,$$

from which

$$\frac{x^3 - 1}{\sqrt{x^3}} = 0 \,, \quad x^3 = 1 \,,$$

which admits the only real solution

$$x = 1 \,.$$

Therefore the point of intersection with the abscissa axis is

$$P_1 = (1, 0) \,.$$

The graph of the function cannot intersecate the ordinate axis because the value $x = 0$ is excluded from the domain. The intersection point with the x axis found is shown in figure 8.1.

Because of the domain the function can be neither even nor odd. For the study of the sign of the function we solve the inequality

$$\sqrt{x^3} - \frac{1}{\sqrt{x^3}} > 0 \,,$$

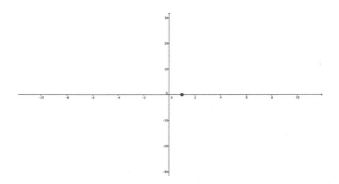

Figure 8.1: Points belonging to the graph of the function $f(x)$.

i.e.

$$\frac{x^3 - 1}{\sqrt{x^3}} > 0 \, .$$

The denominator is always positive in the function domain, while the numerator is positive if

$$x^3 > 1 \, ,$$

i.e.

$$x > 1.$$

The sign of the function follows the pattern shown in figure 8.2.

1

$x^3 - 1 > 0$	$-$	$+$
$\sqrt{x^3} > 0$	$+$	$+$
$\frac{x^3-1}{\sqrt{x^3}} > 0$	$-$	$+$

Figure 8.2: Sign of the function $f(x)$.

The excluded areas of the Cartesian plane are shown in figure 8.3.

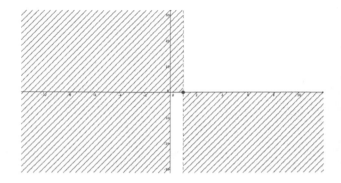

Figure 8.3: Excluded areas for the graph of the function $f(x)$.

The derivative of the function

$$f(x) = x^{3/2} - x^{-3/2} \, ,$$

can be calculated easily

$$f'(x) = \frac{3}{2}x^{1/2} + \frac{3}{2}x^{-5/2} = \frac{3}{2}\left(x^{1/2} + x^{-5/2}\right) \, ,$$

or also

$$f'(x) = \frac{3}{2}\sqrt{x} + \frac{3}{2\sqrt{x^5}} \, .$$

For the study of its sign we need to solve the inequality

$$\frac{3}{2}\sqrt{x} + \frac{3}{2\sqrt{x^5}} > 0 \,,$$

i.e.

$$\sqrt{x} + \frac{1}{\sqrt{x^5}} > 0 \,, \qquad \frac{x^3 + 1}{\sqrt{x^5}} > 0 \,,$$

indeed

$$\sqrt{x^5} \cdot \sqrt{x} = x^{5/2} \cdot x^{1/2} = x^3 \,.$$

The first member denominator is always positive, while the numerator is positive if

$$x^3 > -1 \,,$$

equivalent to

$$x > -1 \,.$$

The sign of the derivative of the function follows the pattern shown in figure 8.4.

$$-1$$

$x^3 + 1 > 0$	$-$	$+$
$\sqrt{x^5} > 0$	$+$	$+$
$\dfrac{x^3+1}{\sqrt{x^5}} > 0$	$-$	$+$

Figure 8.4: Sign of the function $f'(x)$.

Taking into account the domain that imposes $x > 0$, we observe that the first derivative of $f(x)$ is always positive for every $x \in D$ and therefore the function is always increasing. We calculate now the limit

$$\lim_{x \to +\infty} f(x) = \lim_{x \to +\infty} \left(\sqrt{x^3} - \frac{1}{\sqrt{x^3}} \right) = +\infty \,,$$

which shows that the function does not admit horizontal asymptotes. We then calculate

$$
\begin{aligned}
\lim_{x \to +\infty} \frac{f(x)}{x} &= \lim_{x \to +\infty} \frac{1}{x} \left(\sqrt{x^3} - \frac{1}{\sqrt{x^3}} \right) \\
&= \lim_{x \to +\infty} \left(\frac{x^{3/2}}{x} - \frac{1}{x\sqrt{x^3}} \right) \\
&= \lim_{x \to +\infty} x^{1/2} = +\infty
\end{aligned}
$$

and there are also no oblique asymptotes. It remains to verify the limit for x which tends to 0, a point excluded from the domain, which can only be calculated from the right, because we cannot tend to 0 from the left due to the domain requirements. We have

$$\lim_{x \to 0^+} f(x) = \lim_{x \to 0^+} \left(\sqrt{x^3} - \frac{1}{\sqrt{x^3}} \right) = -\infty \,,$$

so the line of equation

$$x = 0$$

represents a vertical asymptote. We calculate the second derivative of the function

$$f(x) = x^{3/2} - x^{-3/2},$$

as follows

$$
\begin{aligned}
f''(x) &= \frac{d}{dx} f'(x) = \frac{d}{dx} \left(\frac{3}{2} \left(x^{1/2} + x^{-5/2} \right) \right) \\
&= \frac{3}{2} \frac{d}{dx} \left(x^{1/2} + x^{-5/2} \right) \\
&= \frac{3}{2} \left(\frac{1}{2} x^{-1/2} - \frac{5}{2} x^{-7/2} \right) \\
&= \frac{3}{2x^{7/2}} \left(\frac{1}{2} x^3 - \frac{5}{2} \right) = \frac{3}{4x^3 \sqrt{x}} \left(x^3 - 5 \right).
\end{aligned}
$$

We study the sign of the second derivative of $f(x)$ by solving the inequality

$$\frac{3}{4x^3 \sqrt{x}} \left(x^3 - 5 \right) > 0,$$

from which, eliminating the positive factors,

$$x^3 - 5 > 0\,,$$

which is equivalent to

$$x > 5^{1/3}\,,$$

with

$$5^{1/3} \simeq 1.710\,.$$

The function has an inflection point at

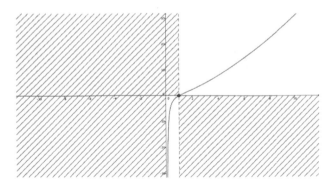

Figure 8.5: Plot of the function $f(x)$.

$$x = 5^{1/3}\,,$$

with ordinate

$$f(5^{1/3}) = 5^{1/2} - 5^{-1/2} \simeq 1.789\,,$$

so that

$$F_1 = \left(5^{1/3}, 5^{1/2} - 5^{-1/2}\right) \simeq (1.710, 1.789)\,.$$

The function has downward concavity for

$$x < 5^{1/3}$$

and upwards for

$$x > 5^{1/3}\,.$$

The function graph can be qualitatively plotted as shown in figure 8.5.

Exercise 9

Perform the study of the following function

$$f(x) = \sqrt{\frac{x}{x-2}}$$

and plot a qualitative graph on a Cartesian plane of axes (x, y) where $y = f(x)$. The domain of the function can be found by solving the system

$$\begin{cases} x - 2 \neq 0 \\ \frac{x}{x-2} \geq 0 \end{cases}$$

From the first equation we have

$$x \neq 2\,,$$

while to solve the inequality we need to study the sign of both numerator and denominator. The numerator is positive if

$$x > 0\,,$$

while the denominator is positive if

$$x > 2\,.$$

The sign of the ratio is shown in the diagram of figure 9.1.
The function

$$\frac{x}{x-2}$$

is positive or null for

$$x \leq 0 \quad \text{or} \quad x > 2\,.$$

	0		2	
$x > 0$	$-$	$+$		$+$
$x - 2 > 0$	$-$	$-$		$+$
$\frac{x}{x-2} > 0$	$+$	$-$		$+$

Figure 9.1: Sign of the function $\frac{x}{x-2}$.

The domain can be written as

$$D = \{x \in \mathbb{R} : x \leq 0 \text{ or } x > 2\}.$$

For the points of intersection with the abscissa axis we solve the system

$$\begin{cases} y = 0 \\ y = \sqrt{\frac{x}{x-2}} \end{cases},$$

i.e.

$$\sqrt{\frac{x}{x-2}} = 0 \,.$$

The solution is

$$x = 0 \,,$$

therefore the point of intersection with the abscissa axis is the origin

$$P_1 = (0,0) \,.$$

which is also the point of intersection with the ordinate axis. This point is shown in figure 9.2. The function does not have a symmetric domain with respect to the ordinate axis therefore it cannot be an even or odd function. To study the sign of the function, we solve the inequality

$$\sqrt{\frac{x}{x-2}} > 0 \,,$$

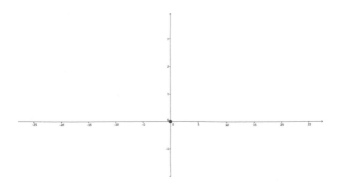

Figure 9.2: Points belonging to the graph of the function $f(x)$.

which is always satisfied except for $x = 0$ for which the function is null. It is possible to exclude some areas in the Cartesian plane, as shown in figure 9.4.

The derivative of the function

$$f(x) = \sqrt{\frac{x}{x-2}} = \left(\frac{x}{x-2}\right)^{1/2}$$

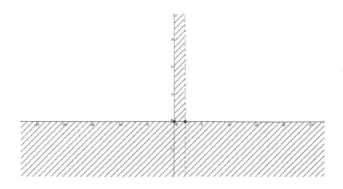

Figure 9.3: Excluded areas for the graph of the function $f(x)$.

is

$$f'(x) = \frac{1}{2}\left(\frac{x}{x-2}\right)^{-1/2} \cdot \frac{d}{dx}\left(\frac{x}{x-2}\right)$$

$$= \frac{1}{2}\left(\frac{x}{x-2}\right)^{-1/2} \frac{x-2-x}{(x-2)^2}$$

$$= \left(\frac{x-2}{x}\right)^{1/2} \frac{-1}{(x-2)^2} = -\frac{1}{\sqrt{x}\,(x-2)^{2-1/2}}$$

$$= -\frac{1}{\sqrt{x}\,(x-2)^{3/2}} \cdot$$

We observe that this function, i.e. $f'(x)$, is always negative in the domain D, therefore the function

$f(x)$ is always decreasing. We calculate now the limits

$$\lim_{x \to \pm\infty} f(x) = \lim_{x \to \pm\infty} \left(\sqrt{\frac{x}{x-2}} \right) = 1 \,,$$

therefore we have the horizontal asymptote of equation

$$y = 1 \,.$$

It remains to calculate the limit for x which tends to 2 (only from the right, due to the domain)

$$\lim_{x \to 2^+} f(x) = \lim_{x \to 2^+} \left(\sqrt{\frac{x}{x-2}} \right) = +\infty \,,$$

hence the line of equation

$$x = 2$$

represents a vertical asymptote. The second derivative of the function

$$f(x) = \sqrt{\frac{x}{x-2}} = \left(\frac{x}{x-2}\right)^{1/2}$$

is

$$
\begin{aligned}
f''(x) &= \frac{d}{dx}f'(x) = \frac{d}{dx}\left(-\frac{1}{\sqrt{x}\,(x-2)^{3/2}}\right) \\
&= -\frac{d}{dx}\left(\frac{1}{(x(x-2)^3)^{1/2}}\right) \\
&= \frac{(x-2)^3 + 3x(x-2)^2}{2x(x-2)^3\,(x(x-2)^3)^{1/2}} \\
&= \frac{x-2+3x}{2x(x-2)\,(x(x-2)^3)^{1/2}} = \frac{2x-1}{x^{3/2}(x-2)^{5/2}}\, .
\end{aligned}
$$

We study its sign by solving

$$\frac{2x-1}{x^{3/2}(x-2)^{5/2}} > 0\,,$$

or

$$2x - 1 > 0\,,$$

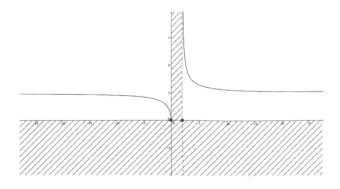

Figure 9.4: Plot of the function $f(x)$.

the other quantities being positive. Finally we have

$$x > \frac{1}{2}.$$

Thanks to the domain

$$D = \left\{ x \in \mathbb{R} : x \leq 0 \text{ or } x > 2 \right\},$$

we conclude that the function $f(x)$ has downward concavity for

$$x \le 0\,,$$

upward concavity for

$$x > 2$$

and has no inflection points. The function graph can be qualitatively plotted as shown in figure 9.4.

Exercise 10

Perform the study of the following function

$$f(x) = x \cdot e^x$$

and plot a qualitative graph on a Cartesian plane of axes (x, y) where $y = f(x)$. The domain of the function is

$$D = \mathbb{R}.$$

To find the points of intersection with the abscissa axis we solve the system

$$\begin{cases} y = 0 \\ y = x \cdot e^x \end{cases},$$

i.e.

$$x \cdot e^x = 0.$$

The exponential is always positive, so that the only solution to this equation is

$$x = 0.$$

The point of intersection with the abscissa axis, and therefore also with the ordinates, is

$$P_1 = (0,0)$$

and it is shown in figure 10.1.

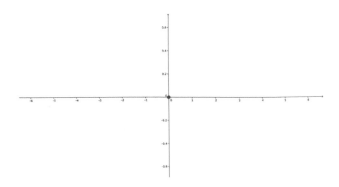

Figure 10.1: Point belonging to the graph of the function $f(x)$.

To verify any symmetries we calculate

$$f(-x) = -x \cdot e^{-x},$$

from which we can conclude that the function $f(x)$ is neither even nor odd. To study the sign of the function, we solve the inequality

$$x \cdot e^x > 0,$$

from which, for what has been said so far,

$$x > 0 \,.$$

The sign of the function follows the pattern shown in figure 10.2.

	0	
$e^x > 0$	$+$	$+$
$x > 0$	$-$	$+$
$\frac{x+1}{x-1} > 0$	$-$	$+$

Figure 10.2: Sign of the function $f(x)$.

We can exclude some areas of the Cartesian plane, as shown in figure 10.3.

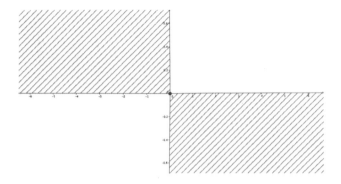

Figure 10.3: Excluded areas for the graph of the function $f(x)$.

The derivative of the function

$$f(x) = x \cdot e^x$$

is

$$f'(x) = e^x + xe^x = e^x(1 + x),$$

for the study of its sign we solve the inequality

$$e^x(1 + x) > 0,$$

from which

$$x > -1 \,.$$

The trend of the sign of the derivative of $f(x)$ and therefore the monotony of the function itself are shown in figure 10.4.

$$-1$$

$e^x > 0$	$+$	$+$
$(x + 1) > 0$	$-$	$+$
$f'(x) = \frac{x+1}{x-1} > 0$	$-$	$+$
$f(x)$	$\searrow$	$\nearrow$

Figure 10.4: Sign of the function $f'(x)$.

The function $f(x)$ is decreasing for $x < -1$, increasing for $x > -1$, and has a relative minimum for $x = -1$. The ordinate of the minimum point is

$$f(-1) = -e^{-1} = -\frac{1}{e} \simeq -0.368$$

and the minimum point is

$$m = \left(-1, -\frac{1}{e}\right) \simeq (-1, -0.368).$$

For the search of asymptotes we calculate the limits

$$\lim_{x \to +\infty} f(x) = \lim_{x \to +\infty} (x \cdot e^x) = +\infty$$

and

$$\begin{aligned}
\lim_{x \to -\infty} f(x) &= \lim_{x \to -\infty} (x \cdot e^x) = \lim_{x \to +\infty} \left(-x \cdot e^{-x}\right) \\
&= -\lim_{x \to +\infty} \frac{x}{e^x} = 0,
\end{aligned}$$

we therefore have the horizontal asymptote on the left of equation

$$y = 0.$$

We calculate the second derivative of the function

$$f(x) = x \cdot e^x \,,$$

i.e.

$$
\begin{aligned}
f''(x) &= \frac{d}{dx} f'(x) = \frac{d}{dx} \left(e^x + xe^x \right) \\
&= e^x + e^x + xe^x = e^x(2 + x) \,,
\end{aligned}
$$

which is positive if

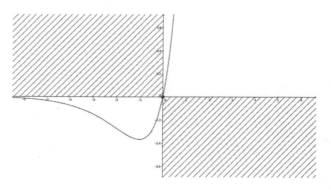

Figure 10.5: Plot of the function $f(x)$.

$$e^x(2 + x) > 0 \,,$$

or also if

$$x > -2\,.$$

The function $f(x)$ has downward concavity for $x < -2$, upward for $x > -2$ and has an inflection in $x = -2$ with ordinate

$$f(-2) = -2e^{-2} = -\frac{2}{e^2} \simeq -0.271\,.$$

The inflection point is

$$F_1 = l\left(-2, -\frac{2}{e^2}\right) \simeq (-2, -0.271)\,.$$

The graph of the function can be plotted qualitatively as shown in figure 10.5.

Exercise 11

Perform the study of the following function

$$f(x) = (1 + e^x)^{-1}$$

and plot a qualitative graph on a Cartesian plane of axes (x, y) where $y = f(x)$. The function can also be written as

$$f(x) = \frac{1}{1 + e^x}$$

and its domain is

$$D = \mathbb{R},$$

in fact the denominator can never be zero as the exponential is always positive. To find the points of intersection with the abscissa axis, we solve the system

$$\begin{cases} y = 0 \\ y = \frac{1}{1+e^x} \end{cases},$$

i.e.

$$\frac{1}{1 + e^x} = 0.$$

This equation does not admit solutions therefore there are no points of intersection with the abscissa axis. we solve the system for the point of intersection with the ordinate axis

$$\begin{cases} x = 0 \\ y = \frac{1}{1+e^x} \end{cases},$$

which leads to

$$y = \frac{1}{1 + e^0} = \frac{1}{2}.$$

The point of intersection with the y axis is therefore

$$P_1 = \left(0, \frac{1}{2}\right)$$

and it is shown in figure 11.1.

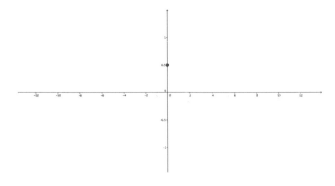

Figure 11.1: Point belonging to the graph of the function $f(x)$.

We calculate

$$f(-x) = \frac{1}{1 + e^{-x}} \, ,$$

which shows that the function is neither even nor odd. To study the sign of the function, we solve the inequality

$$\frac{1}{1 + e^x} > 0 \, ,$$

who is always satisfied. It is possible to exclude from the graph the entire lower half plane for which $y < 0$, as shown in figure 11.2.

The derivative of the function

$$f(x) = \frac{1}{1 + e^x}$$

is

$$f'(x) = -\frac{e^x}{(1 + e^x)^2} \, .$$

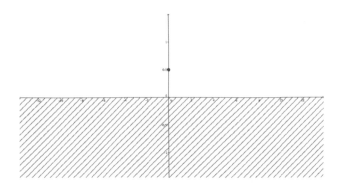

Figure 11.2: Excluded areas for the graph of the function $f(x)$.

To study its sign, we solve the inequality

$$-\frac{e^x}{(1+e^x)^2} > 0 \,,$$

which does not admit solutions, in fact the fraction has always positive numerator and denominator. The $f(x)$ function is therefore always decreasing and has no relative maxima or minima. The trend is summarized in the diagram of figure 11.3.

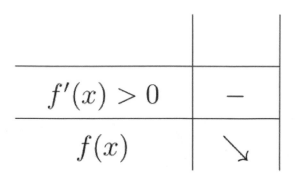

Figure 11.3: Performance of the $f'(x)$ function.

We calculate the limits

$$\lim_{x \to +\infty} f(x) = \lim_{x \to +\infty} \left(\frac{1}{1 + e^x} \right) = 0 \,,$$

$$\lim_{x \to -\infty} f(x) = \lim_{x \to -\infty} \left(\frac{1}{1 + e^x} \right) = 1 \,,$$

there are therefore two horizontal asymptotes, one on the right of equation

$$y = 0$$

and the other on the left of equation

$$y = 1 \, .$$

The second derivative of the function

$$f(x) = \frac{1}{1 + e^x}$$

can be calculated as

$$
\begin{aligned}
f''(x) &= \frac{d}{dx} f'(x) = \frac{d}{dx} \left(-\frac{e^x}{(1 + e^x)^2} \right) \\
&= -\frac{e^x (1 + e^x)^2 - 2(1 + e^x) e^x e^x}{(1 + e^x)^4} \\
&= -\frac{e^x (1 + e^x - 2e^x)}{(1 + e^x)^3} = -\frac{e^x (1 - e^x)}{(1 + e^x)^3} \, .
\end{aligned}
$$

We study its sign by solving the inequality

$$-\frac{e^x (1 - e^x)}{(1 + e^x)^3} > 0 \, ,$$

or

$$1 - e^x < 0 \, , \quad e^x > 1 \, ,$$

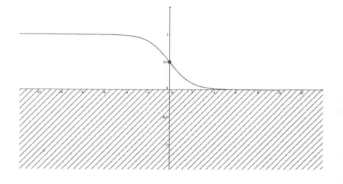

Figure 11.4: Plot of the function $f(x)$.

i.e.

$$x > 0\,.$$

The function therefore has downward concavity for $x < 0$, upward for $x > 0$ and has an inflection point of abscissa $x = 0$. The corresponding ordinate is

$$f(0) = \frac{1}{1 + e^0} = \frac{1}{2}\,,$$

therefore the inflection point is

$$F_1 = \left(0, \frac{1}{2}\right) .$$

The qualitative graph is shown in figure 11.4.

Exercise 12

Perform the study of the following function

$$f(x) = (1 - e^{-x})^{-1}$$

and plot a qualitative graph on a Cartesian plane of axes (x, y) where $y = f(x)$. The function can also be written as

$$f(x) = \frac{1}{1 - e^{-x}} \,.$$

For the domain it is necessary to ask

$$1 - e^{-x} \neq 0, \quad \frac{1}{e^x} \neq 1, \quad e^x \neq 1,$$

from which

$$x \neq 0 \,.$$

The domain is

$$D = \mathbb{R} - \{0\} \,.$$

For the points of intersection with the abscissa axis we solve the system

$$\begin{cases} y = 0 \\ y = \frac{1}{1-e^{-x}} \end{cases} ,$$

i.e.

$$\frac{1}{1 - e^{-x}} = 0 \,.$$

This equation does not admit solutions, so there are no points of intersection with the abscissa axis. The graph of the function cannot intersect the ordinate axis because $x = 0$ is a point excluded from the domain. There are therefore no points of intersection with either of the two Cartesian axes. We calculate

$$f(-x) = \frac{1}{1 - e^x}$$

and we can conclude that the function is neither even nor odd. To study the sign of the function, we solve the inequality

$$\frac{1}{1 - e^{-x}} > 0, \quad 1 - e^{-x} > 0, \quad \frac{1}{e^x} < 1,$$

from which

$$e^x > 1, \quad x > 0,$$

The sign of the function is shown in figure 12.1. The areas of the Cartesian plane that can be excluded are shown in figure 12.2.

The derivative of the function

$$f(x) = \frac{1}{1 - e^{-xx}}$$

$$0$$

$1 > 0$	$+$	$+$
$1 - e^{-x} > 0$	$-$	$+$
$(1 - e^{-x})^{-1} > 0$	$-$	$+$

Figure 12.1: Sign of the function $f(x)$.

is

$$f'(x) = -\frac{e^{-x}}{(1 - e^{-x})^2} \cdot$$

To study its sign, we solve the inequality

$$-\frac{e^{-x}}{(1 - e^{-x})^2} > 0 \,,$$

which does not admit solutions, in fact the fraction is always positive. The $f(x)$ function is always decreasing and has no relative maxima or

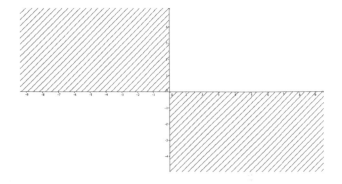

Figure 12.2: Excluded areas for the graph of the function $f(x)$.

minima. The trend is summarized in figure 12.3.

We calculate now the two limits

$$\lim_{x \to +\infty} f(x) = \lim_{x \to +\infty} \left(\frac{1}{1 - e^{-x}} \right) = 1 \,,$$

$$\lim_{x \to -\infty} f(x) = \lim_{x \to -\infty} \left(\frac{1}{1 - e^{-x}} \right) = 0 \,,$$

There are two horizontal asymptotes, one on the right with equation

$$y = 1$$

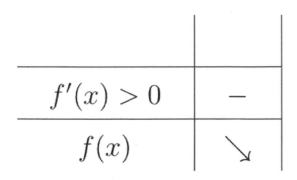

Figure 12.3: Sign of the function $f'(x)$.

and the other on the left with equation

$$y = 0\,.$$

We must also calculate the limits to the point excluded from the domain. We have

$$\lim_{x \to 0^+} f(x) = \lim_{x \to 0^+} \left(\frac{1}{1 - e^{-x}} \right) = +\infty\,,$$

$$\lim_{x \to 0^-} f(x) = \lim_{x \to 0^-} \left(\frac{1}{1 - e^{-x}} \right) = -\infty\,,$$

We calculate the second derivative of the function

$$f(x) = \frac{1}{1 - e^{-x}} \, ,$$

obtaining

$$f''(x) = \frac{d}{dx} f'(x) = \frac{d}{dx} \left(-\frac{e^{-x}}{(1 - e^{-x})^2} \right)$$

$$= -\frac{-e^{-x}(1 - e^{-x})^2 - 2(1 - e^{-x})e^{-x}e^{-x}}{(1 - e^{-x})^4}$$

$$= -\frac{e^{-x}\left(-1 + e^{-x} - 2e^{-x} \right)}{(1 - e^{-x})^3}$$

$$= \frac{e^{-x}\left(1 + e^{-x} \right)}{(1 - e^{-x})^3}$$

and we study its sign by solving the inequality

$$\frac{e^{-x}\left(1 + e^{-x} \right)}{(1 - e^{-x})^3} > 0 \, ,$$

or

$$(1 - e^{-x})^3 > 0 \, , \quad 1 - e^{-x} > 0 \, , \quad e^{-x} < 1 \, ,$$

from which

$$e^x > 1 \, , \quad x > 0 \, .$$

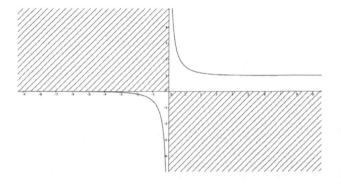

Figure 12.4: Plot of the function $f(x)$.

The function therefore has downward concavity for $x < 0$ and upward concavity for $x > 0$. The qualitative graph is shown in figure 12.4.

Made in the USA
Middletown, DE
25 September 2021